Empath Armor

How to Ground, Cleanse, and Protect Your Energy as a Sensitive Person

By: Dr. April Darley

Table of Contents

Introduction

Have you been described as overly sensitive? Do you take on the feelings of others as if they were your own? Do you suffer from anxiety or depression? These are common symptoms that could mean you are an Empath!

I decided to write this book after being asked to speak to a group interested in holistic and alternative medicine. After this speech, it became clear to me that so many people were needlessly suffering because they didn't have the proper tools to keep themselves feeling grounded, protected and safe from outside energies and influences.

 Through thousands of hours providing Neuro-Emotional Technique (N.E.T.) to clients, I began to identify certain patterns that were common to a group of people known as Empaths" or Highly Sensitive People. Empaths have certain personality traits that we will discuss later, but these caring, loving, and giving individuals are often taken advantage of and are still carrying wounds from their experiences. It's my desire to offer some basic techniques that will strengthen you, and help you interact with others without feeling drained, used, and hopeless. If you've been searching for answers and a better way to live your life, then this book is for you!

In this book, we will cover topics including:

-What is an Empath and why you might be one

-Using divine energy to protect and cleanse your personal energy

-Find out which gemstones and crystals are good for grounding, protection, and cleansing

-How to cut cords between you and others to avoid having your energy drained

-Using essential oils for energetic health

- How to use flower essences to strengthen your personal boundaries

-Easy at-home techniques to rejuvenate your energy

-Meditation and Visualization techniques to keep your energy clear

What Is an Empath?

My personal definition of an Empath is an individual who is loving, giving, and has a "healing" energy or way about them. It doesn't matter what your occupation may be (i.e. what you do for money), but your "job" is often to help people heal in some way. I've had Empath clients who were engineers, hair stylists, mechanics, retail sales associates etc. They all had certain personality traits that identified them as an Empath, and therefore, many of the same issues in their personal lives.

Positive traits of empaths include:

- Kind
- Compassionate
- Intuitive
- Great Listeners
- Problem Solvers
- Creative
- Giving
- Animal lovers
- Natural healers
- Natural counselors

Empaths make the best friends ever! You naturally give great advice, and your friends, family or co-workers often seek you out to talk about their problems. Because you're a healer, you naturally want to help. The problem? These people can leave you feeling drained, sad, depressed and just plain yucky. Reasons for this include not setting proper boundaries, and not protecting or cleansing your personal energy (more on this later).

If your personal energy is not protected or cleansed regularly, this sets you up to experience the following symptoms:

- Anxiety
- Depression
- Self-Isolation (as a coping mechanism)
- Weight gain
- Difficulty saying no
- Rescuing others
- People pleasing
- Giving until you're empty, but feeling selfish if you receive
- Low self-esteem
- Taking on the emotional or physical pain of others and being unable to distinguish it as foreign energy

Keeping Yourself Grounded

One way to avoid the negative symptoms we just discussed is to ground yourself. Grounding is the practice of making sure that you're connected and aware of your physical self in addition to your spiritual and energetic self.

When you're aware of what your own energy and physical body feel like, then you can determine if you've picked up energy that is "not your own". You see, Empaths act like a sponge soaking up the ills and emotions of other people. For example, have you ever been around someone with pain in their body and then you started having the same pain shortly after? If so, then you've most likely absorbed their ill energy.

7

You'll do this unconsciously because of your desire to help people heal. You don't consciously WANT to take their pain, but you just can't help it. Grounding can help you block this sponge effect.

If you haven't absorbed someone's physical pain, then you may be absorbing their emotional pain. Have you ever been in a great mood until talking to someone who wasn't? Afterward, your good mood evaporates, and you feel heavy, tired, and maybe even depressed while they walk away feeling much better. This is because you were an emotional dumping ground for their yucky energy!

Grounding can keep you feeling centered even when there's chaos around you. It can also keep you from unconsciously giving AWAY your energy in attempt to heal or make someone feel better. It serves as the strong foundation on which you begin to rebuild yourself.

I'm going to provide you with a few simple techniques that you can use to ground yourself. Everyone will resonate to a different technique, so please choose one or two that make the best sense for your lifestyle and beliefs. The most important part of grounding includes doing it! The more you practice grounding, the faster and easier it will become.

Gemstones and Crystals for Grounding

Gemstones and Crystals (I will often use these terms interchangeably) are great for someone who is deeply connected to the earth and resonates with natural healing. There are many stones that could be used for this purpose, but

I chose a few of my favorites. The stones that I'll recommend can be purchased in raw or polished forms, can be worn as jewelry, carried in your pockets, a pouch or even your bra (this choice is popular for ladies with no pockets or to keep your stones close to your heart)!

1) Onyx
- Root chakra stone
- Increases your willpower and ability to focus
- Increases your ability to resist and persist
- Helps realign your attention and perception to your own activities
- Helps break bad habits including addictions

Onyx is a great gemstone to have because it helps you to feel safe and secure in both yourself and your surroundings. This is often an area of great difficulty for Empaths. Quite frequently, a traumatic childhood background begins a cycle of feeling unsafe. First, it was feeling unsafe in their home environment. Then, this lack of foundational safety expands in the unconscious and subconscious brains to include other relationships and environments such as school, work, friends etc. Once the unconscious and subconscious brains detect a perceived threat, a cascade of chemicals causes a reaction in your nervous system and prepare to engage the threat with fight, flight or freeze. Suddenly, you're feeling anxious, panicky, and your conscious brain doesn't have a clue what's going on. This cascade is why many Empaths feel anxious and they don't know why because it isn't logical.

Since Onyx is a grounding stone, it helps your mental concentration and focus. This focus allows you to figure out what emotions and energy belong to you and what doesn't. It helps you stand your ground, stay in your power, and break the habit of people pleasing. Since Empaths were often placed into environments where their brain and body were placed in survival mode, people pleasing became a necessary way to ensure survival and acceptance. Later, feelings of unworthiness make it difficult to say NO, and you feel guilty if you aren't people pleasing. Since you aren't being true to yourself when people pleasing occurs, it can often leave you feeling drained, resentful, and used as a result. Onyx helps you break patterns related to people pleasing and other addictive or dependent behaviors. It also corresponds to the root chakra which governs the areas of safety, security, survival, and family. Empaths often need extra support in these areas.

2) **Hematite**
- Good for mental organization
- Helps balance mind/body/spirit
- Boosts self-esteem and confidence
- Strengthens your connection with the earth making you feel safe and secure
- Helps you to avoid absorbing the energy of others

My first experience with Hematite came when I was in medical school. While there, I was exposed to people from all over the country with different ways of thinking, but similar interests. For the first time in my life, I was surrounded by my tribe! After classes and studying, we would explore metaphysical topics such as energy work, herbal medicines, chakras, gemstone and crystal healing. While we were expanding ourselves in every possible way, I began to open-up intuitively. As my crown chakra opened, I would often become disoriented, dizzy, and felt like I wasn't fully anchored in my body. Simply put, I wasn't grounded.

Being ungrounded can cause you to feel "spacey" or unfocused. When my crown chakra would open suddenly, I would feel like my head was swirling and I would even lose my balance at times. Hematite helps you keep a clear head and is a very powerful grounding stone. When you hold it, it even feels heavy in your hand! This is powerful grounding medicine. Hematite is often fashioned into jewelry which is great to wear at work or home for extra support. In school, I would wear a hematite bracelet, rings and occasionally an anklet to keep myself grounded. After I learned to control my energy better, I no longer felt like I was going to float away!

Hematite is great for the root chakra and can assist in making you feel safe and secure while boosting your confidence and focus. It's a highly protective stone keeping you from unconsciously absorbing the emotions of others. This is important to counteract the sponge-like tendency of an Empath to take on the emotions and pain of others that don't belong to you. Hematite makes great Empath armor!

3) Garnet
- Promotes emotional stability
- Allows you to live your own life without fear
- Helps you pursue your passions with confidence
- Provides courage, support, and strength

Because Empaths often have difficult childhoods, building relationships that involve trust and love can be challenging. Garnet helps provide emotional stability and foster relationships that YOU build with mutual love and respect. It acts like a stone of optimism when it comes to love by helping you repair faulty patterns of love from past romances and family dynamics. Empaths often need help repairing their ideas of SELF-LOVE as well! Because it connects both the root and heart chakras, Garnet increases your self-esteem by helping you stay grounded in love. It also helps deflect negative energy sent your way serving as a form of protection as well. Garnet regulates your energy flow keeping you grounded while feeling protected psychically and emotionally.

4) Smoky Quartz
- Grounds your essence in reality
- Helps you prioritize your needs and wants
- A good balancer of physical and psychic energy

Smoky Quartz is one of the best tools in your gemstone repertoire! Not only does it ground, but it also cleanses and shields. Smoky Quartz as a grounding stone, assists in letting go of negative emotions such as fear, jealousy, and anger from your past. By neutralizing negativity that you've collected from others, it helps you separate what's yours from what belongs to others. In this way, you're better able to function with clarity.

Empaths don't often consider their needs as important as the needs of others. It's a common trait of Empaths that they would rather GIVE than receive. It can make you feel selfish if you receive, and you may not feel worthy of receiving the same loving care and attention that you so freely give to others. Smoky Quartz can help you do this without feeling guilt. After all, YOU are important as a healer! If you don't take care of yourself, then you can't help others!

5) **Red Jasper**
- Helps you to focus and get organized
- Helps you to focus and begin creative activities
- Stabilizes aura and grounds
- Increases stamina

Red jasper can help you feel empowered again especially if you've felt victimized or dominated by others. This often happens when Empaths engage in romantic relationships with an incompatible person, or if your family dynamic had an overbearing parent. As a survival mechanism, Empaths learned to engage in people pleasing, or to sacrifice their own wants and needs. Red jasper helps rebuild your confidence if you've been bullied or harassed by others.

In addition, it stimulates your creative passions and helps you rediscover those creative talents that you may have suppressed. I can't tell you the number of clients I've had in their 30's-50's who come into my office feeling lost. They're unhappy with their current job, but don't know what to do instead. Quite often, their parents discouraged them from following careers in the arts by scaring them into thinking those pursuits would lead to poverty. Many clients had parents who refused to pay for their college education unless it was in something that would lead to "a good career" such as business or medicine. This led to frustration and a longing that was present years later from being denied their heart's desire to create. Red Jasper helps you regain that passion for expressing yourself creatively, and because it's a grounding stone, feeling safe in doing it.

6) **Black Obsidian**
- Helps release stored negative energies
- Helps you move forward if you're feeling stuck
- Assists in meditation to help you feel grounded and problem solve

Have you noticed a pattern that the gemstones that I've mentioned so far are either black or red? This is because they correspond to the root chakra. Black Obsidian helps you feel grounded in meditation with the clarity to solve problems that are keeping you feeling stuck. It helps you release stored negativity in a safe way relieving tension, restlessness, and irritability. If you're prone to nightmares or anxiousness at night, then keeping Black Obsidian near your bedside keeps you feeling grounded and safe.

Essential Oils for Grounding

Essential oils can be used in a variety of ways. They can be diluted and worn on your skin, placed in a diffuser, or used in aromatherapy jewelry throughout the day. Scent is powerful and can serve as a reminder to keep yourself focused and feeling safe. If you would like to wear them on your skin, make sure that you dilute the oils approximately 1 drop in 1 teaspoon of a carrier oil such as coconut, apricot, grapeseed, almond or olive oil. This is a 1% dilution. You can increase the strength of your formula by adding more drops per teaspoon. Most essential oils should not be placed directly on the skin without dilution. Always test a small patch of your skin to check for any potential reactions.

It's no coincidence that most grounding oils are made from trees. Being grounded means being stable physically, mentally, emotionally, and spiritually. It allows you to be fully present in your life. Because they tend to be rather potent, you may want to mix them in a blend with lighter scents such as citrus or florals. Here are a few basic grounding oils to start.

1) Cedarwood
- Feeling isolated or lonely
- The need to control your environment and others
- Helps you release anger

When you feel the need to control every aspect of your life, it can lead to anger and frustration if circumstances and people aren't doing exactly what you want. It's a hard lesson to learn sometimes, but we can only control our reaction to situations. What other people do and say is ultimately their free will choice. Anger can arise when things aren't going our way. Cedarwood can help you release the need for control, and the resulting anger that's been building. If you're feeling alone and misunderstood, then Cedarwood can help you integrate socially. Empaths will often isolate themselves as a protective mechanism. Cedarwood helps you achieve the level of grounding and protection you need to feel safe socializing with others.

2) **Patchouli**
- Relaxes the body
- Helps you let go of shame
- Promotes self-love and healthy body image

If you've ever been made to feel like you weren't good enough in the past, then Patchouli can help. This oil would be especially good if you have a history of body-shaming or sexual abuse. Patchouli helps you let go of stored shame and finally accept yourself. It allows you to view your body as a gift and worthy of being your spirit's home. It uplifts your mood and resolves depression. Patchouli can also calm down the sympathetic nervous system shifting you out of fight or flight and into rest and relaxation.

3) **Cypress**
- Fear
- Trouble letting go
- Feeling blocked spiritually

Cypress is great if you're feeling like you can't quite connect with your spiritual self. It helps you flow into your life and let go of rigid thinking. If you're in a time of transition such as divorce, grief, new job, new marriage or child, then Cypress helps relieve the tension and stress of stepping into your new life. If you're feeling sadness and grief due to your transition, then Cypress transmutes that into comfort and support.

4) Sandalwood

- Helps you re-focus on spiritual pursuits rather than materialistic
- Emotional grounding
- Relieves worry and anxiety

I was hesitant to include Sandalwood in this section, but it's an excellent grounding oil. The problem? It's being drastically overharvested and is in danger of extinction in some areas. Because of its popularity, some areas have been overharvesting without re-planting. Other species of Sandalwood, such as Australian Sandalwood, are being used to avoid overharvesting and extinction. I urge you to make sure that your supplier of Sandalwood is practicing ethical harvesting and replanting methods. If you're unsure, then choose another one of the oils in this section instead.

Sandalwood is considered a sacred oil and will open the crown chakra to connect you with spirit. It increases your clarity and mental focus while calming your worries and fears. Sandalwood also increases your sense of stability and restores your capacity to trust.

5) Angelica

- Helps you make decisions from the heart
- Helps you get in tune with what you really want
- Calming and balancing

Angelica helps restore your sense of safety and stability, especially if you've had a traumatic background. Because it opens the heart, Angelica can put you in touch with what YOU really want instead of trying to please others. It takes courage to face your fears, admit what you want, and then go after it. Angelica allows you to make the decision of your heart and not your head. It helps you commit to your own dreams, wants, and needs without fear of letting others down. Angelica is named after the Archangel Michael who is all about protection, courage and strength. It gives you a feeling of angelic comfort to be your true self.

6) Myrrh
- Helps establish harmony between physical and spiritual pursuits
- Calms the mind
- Soothes anxious thoughts

Myrrh helps you feel grounded by strengthening the connection between the crown and root chakras. It helps a mind racing with worry and anxiety to slow down and stabilize. If you're worried about the future, then Myrrh helps you relax and stay in the present moment. It helps you let go of material fears such as money and work. Instead, it connects you with what's truly important in life.

Other Grounding Techniques

Another grounding technique involves visualization and calling in divine energy. If you like to work with God, Angels, Buddha, Jesus, Source, Universe, etc., then this technique may appeal to you.

The Bubble of Divine Light

Simply ask to be covered in divine healing light. It's that easy! We often get too busy and forget to ask for what we need, or we simply don't because we think it's selfish. But guess what? The Divine (God, Source, Universe, Creator) is just waiting on YOU to ask for help! So, ask away and start visualizing!

In this technique, the color of the light can be whatever makes you feel safe and protected. Some common colors are white, pink, gold, green or purple. The shape can be whatever you like, but many people just surround themselves with a bubble or cylinder. If you work with Angels, then Archangel Sandalphon who uses a turquoise colored light can assist you. In addition, I also ask that I be grounded deeply into the earth and anchored to the divine source. This way, I can pull up a deep sense of grounding from the earth and a deep sense of love and protection from the divine. If you're new to grounding and visualization, then you may have to repeat this visualization a few times a day especially if you're still feeling drained at the end of the day. I try to do this visualization before I leave the house to make sure that I'm ready for my day.

Roots into the Earth

Another visualization technique involves grounding yourself solely to the earth. This is a great meditation to do if you work with the public or in the healing arts. Doing this before each client, or at the beginning of the day helps you feel connected to the Earth.

Simply sit or lie comfortably. Take several slow and deep breaths. Visualize roots growing from the soles of your feet

19

deep into the earth's core. See the core of the earth as a bubble colored with whatever light you like. Visualize the roots from your feet wrapping around the core and the light from the core flowing up your roots and into your body. If you feel that you've absorbed energy that is not our own, then you can also send that energy back into the core of the earth to release what's been stored within you.

Feet on the Ground

The last grounding technique involves taking off your shoes and simply walking on the ground with your bare feet. This helps you reconnect to the earth and your own energy. The Earth vibrates to a frequency of approximately 783 Hz. Our stressful modern lives and the use of electronics changes our frequency. By walking on the ground, you begin to resonate with the healing frequency of the Earth.

Meditation

In addition to these grounding techniques, I also suggest meditation. In my opinion, there's no right or wrong way to meditate. You can sit up or lie down as you prefer. There are several free apps available for your phone that offer guided meditations, or timed meditations involving only music. Simply choose the one that works best for you on any given day. These apps have meditations ranging from 5 minutes to almost 2 hours! It's easy to start slowly and then work yourself up when you have more time.

Journaling Exercise

As an Empath, it's helpful to REALLY get to know yourself so that you can differentiate your feelings from those of others. Ask yourself the following questions:

-What does it feel like when you're grounded?
-What does being grounded mean to you?
-How would you describe being grounded to others?
- What's the best way you've found to ground yourself?

Now that you know how to ground, let's talk about how to protect yourself.

Protection

The main reason you want to protect your energy is to keep others from siphoning it away. Otherwise, you can be a walking juice box for those people who unconsciously or consciously absorb your energy. Conversely, if you're an Empath and you see someone in need, you may GIVE your energy away in an attempt to help others. By having proper energetic boundaries in place, you can avoid both situations.

Some people don't like the word "protection" because it implies that you're unsafe. Another term that's commonly used is shielding. If you think about energetic protection, it can function like a suit of armor or even an umbrella in the rain. Without it, you're not in danger, but you won't be as comfortable. An energetic umbrella or suit of armor helps you walk around with a little extra insulation if you're in public or crowded situations. This is especially important if your occupation involves dealing with large amounts of people daily such as in retail or healthcare fields.

Another benefit to shielding is that it helps keep you grounded. If your own energy is preserved, then it's not being mixed with the energy of others. This keeps you from acting as an energetic sponge. When your energy is purely your own, you'll be able to handle any emotional issues that arise more easily.

Here's a tip: If you're happy one moment and sad shortly after without any explicable reason, then you've most likely absorbed emotions from someone else. Knowing yourself and your feelings extremely well (i.e. through good grounding, shielding, and introspection) will help you quickly identify when you've absorbed emotions that are not your own so that the energy can be cleansed and released. In this way, you can rebalance yourself quickly.

Shielding or protecting your energy is something you want to do daily. This is especially important before you leave home for work in the morning, or if you're living with someone who drains your energy. The following technique is simple, but it may require a little practice if you're unaccustomed to meditation or visualization practices.

Visualization with Divine Light

This is something that can be done very quickly. I like to do this in the shower to make sure that I'm all set for the day. As with the grounding, use whatever color of light that makes you feel safe and comfortable. Popular choices are white, pink, purple, and green. Simply imagine the light around you in either a bubble or column. It's also great to set the intention that only love and light can enter your bubble and that it will repel anything that would mean you negativity or harm. I like to layer up the colors of light so that I'm extra protected! The exact color or shape of your light can vary on your beliefs and personality. Make it unique just like you! Some people even like to visualize mirrors facing outward so that any negativity directed toward you returns to its sender. If you do this technique, it's a good idea to make sure that you cleanse or bless the energy returning to avoid any negative karma.

If you like to use Angels in your visualization, then here are a few great ones to call in for some extra help.

- **Archangel Michael:** Dark blue light
  - Protection, courage, strength
- **Raphael:** Emerald green light
  - Healing on all levels from known and unknown issues
- **Guardian Angels:** White light
  - Unconditional love, guidance, support
- **Sandalphon:** Turquoise light
  - Grounding to the earth and into spirit

Gemstones and Crystals for Protection

1) Black Tourmaline
- Helps transmute any negative energy coming in and changes it to positive energy
- Helps keep your energy balanced and positive
- Helps shield you from EMF

Black tourmaline is one of my favorite gemstones for protecting against negativity. I have a large chunk on my desk when I'm in session with clients because it will absorb any emotions released, transforming them into positive energy. This is a great stone for those working in the healthcare field, or if you're exposed to less than positive people in your home and work environment. The ability to transform negative to positive is a powerful ally if you're in a leadership position. Black tourmaline helps bring out your innate positive qualities and magnify them for your best advantage. Black tourmaline is also a powerful grounding and cleansing stone like Smoky Quartz. So, you get an additional bonus!

   If you feel like you're around energy vampires, then Black tourmaline helps to protect your energy from being their latest snack! When vampires steal your energy, it can leave you feeling tired, drained, depressed, and lethargic. I recommend keeping a piece with you or wearing it as a bracelet or necklace if possible.

Empaths often have issues with feeling drained due to exposure to EMF (Electro Magnetic Frequency) from computers or other technology. Keeping a piece of black tourmaline in your pocket or on your desk, can help shield you and maintain balanced energy. Black tourmaline releases negative ions to uplift the area around you.

   2)   Tiger's Eye
-   Helps release your fears and anxieties
-   Increases confidence and optimism
-   Increases your focus and strategy

Tiger's eye is a stone that increases your determination and willpower while giving you the confidence to push forward in your life. When our personal aura gets muddied with the energies of others, it can be hard to focus on what we truly want to accomplish. Tiger's eye helps foster wisdom and the ability to strategize effectively. This ability to be observant, wise, and mentally clear helps you pick up on potential threats in your environment and take appropriate action. Knowing who and what to trust is often a big issue for Empaths because of their past experiences. Tiger's eye allows you to regain that inner power to trust your own intuition and judgment about people and experiences. It gives you courage and empowerment so that you no longer feel like a victim of circumstance or allow others to take advantage of you. Tiger's eye is also known as a psychic protector and is used in the practice of Feng Shui to help ward off negative energy that may be directed to you or your business.

3) Amethyst
- Guards against psychic attack
- Transmutes negative energy to love
- Blocks geopathic stress and negative environmental energy
- Helps center and balance one emotionally and calms the mind and nervous system

Amethyst is another one of my favorite gemstones. It can easily be worn as jewelry and serves a variety of purposes. Empaths often feel anxious and frazzled because they have absorbed the energy of others and in general can feel unsafe in many situations. This overall anxiety can activate your sympathetic nervous system (AKA your fight or flight mechanism). Amethyst helps you attain an emotional balance and shifts you back into a parasympathetic or relaxed mode. Because Amethyst helps you center and calm your emotions, it can also protect you from psychic vampires. It helps you to analyze your emotions and to sort out yours from the clutter of others. When you have a clear idea of what's yours, you can better decide whether to act on them. It's associated with the crown chakra and purifies the mind. Pairing Amethyst with Black tourmaline will increase the ability to repel negative people and influences.

In addition to its uplifting and emotional balancing ability, Amethyst helps keep you stable despite what may be going on in your environment. For example, there are certain Empaths who are very sensitive to changes in the Earth. Something called Geopathic stress can occur if you're sensitive to the features of a geographic location. Carrying a piece of Amethyst can help keep you from feeling overwhelmed by changes in the Earth or your environment.

4) Snowflake Obsidian
- Calms fears especially over scarcity
- Helps provide physical, spiritual, and emotional protection
- Blocks negative energy from entering your life
- Helps you recognize harmful or unhealthy patterns

Snowflake Obsidian is another stone that is both grounding and protective. Sometimes, when you feel like you've been making the wrong choices over and over, you tend to get a little depressed. This stone helps you to recognize when you're not making the best choice and gives you the opportunity to learn from the lessons these patterns are trying to teach you. Snowflake Obsidian gives you that little boost you need to end unhealthy patterns once and for all! With newfound clarity and optimism, you're able to see opportunities beyond the challenges and let go of the fear of making positive steps in your life.

If you feel like you've hit rock bottom, or that your life is falling apart, then Snowflake Obsidian keeps you out of that dark place the mind tends to wander. It calms your fear about what seems to be missing in your life, while guiding you towards the inner strength you need to pull through and keep going. This stone helps repel negativity coming your way allowing you to be aware of the source.

5) Labradorite
- Seals your aura to prevent energy leakage
- Strengthens your willpower and provides purpose
- Relaxes an overactive mind

Labradorite is an aura cleanser and seals your aura to prevent energy leakage or vampires draining you. It forms an energy barrier to keep the good in and the bad out! A clean and protected aura allows you to ditch the negative thoughts and bad habits weighing you down. Labradorite increases your spiritual and psychic awareness so that you're better able to protect yourself and determine your true path.

One of the symptoms of having absorbed too much negativity is an overactive mind filled with anxious thoughts. Labradorite also acts like a cleansing stone to detach this negativity from the mind. It's a good idea to end your day with Labradorite especially if you're around a lot of toxic people. It can help you discern who can be trusted in your life and what negativity needs to go.

6) **Fluorite**
- Protects against psychic manipulation
- Wards off negative energy affecting relationships
- Protects against EMF

Fluorite helps you become more organized and focused in your life. It protects you mentally and psychically from those who would seek to manipulate you. It helps you feel whole in both mind and spirit. Fluorite increases the quality and bonds of your most cherished relationships by blocking negative influences that would cause harm or sabotage. With Fluorite, you have stable relationships that are positive and in alignment with your true self.

In addition to protecting your aura, Fluorite is also environmentally protective. Placing it near your computer, tv, or desk at work keeps you from absorbing the ill effects of EMF. When you're sensitive to EMF, you can feel like you have "brain fog", lightheaded, spacey or even tingling in your extremities. Holding a piece of Fluorite can help ground you back into the Earth's energy if you've absorbed too much EMF and are suffering from the results.

Fluorite comes in many different colors and each one has slightly different properties. I encourage you to look at each color and find the right fit for you.

Essential Oils for Protection

Reminder: If you'd like to wear essential oils on your skin, make sure that you dilute the oils approximately 1-2 drops in 1 teaspoon of a carrier oil such as coconut, apricot, grapeseed, jojoba, avocado, almond or olive oil. Most essential oils should not be placed directly on the skin without dilution. Always test a small patch of your skin to check for any potential reactions.

Another method for using essential oils is to make a protection spray. Fill a darkly colored glass bottle with spring water. Amber or cobalt blue are often used to protect the oils from breaking down due to light and heat. Don't use a plastic bottle as the oils will cause the plastic to breakdown. Add a few drops of essential oil to the bottle along with 1-2 tablespoons of a preservative such as witch hazel or alcohol and spray as needed. This method is also great for using the cleansing oils we will discuss in the next section.

1) Rose:
- Opens and uplifts the heart and emotions.
- Helps you feel safe, protected, and nurtured.
- Helps relieve anxiety and depression
- Calms the nervous system

It takes 1 ton of roses to make about 1 oz of pure Rose essential oil. Consequently, it's extremely expensive. You can purchase "absolutes" which have been extracted using a solvent which is cheaper. However, be careful about the type of solvent used and only purchase from a reputable dealer.

Rose absolute will still be over $100 for a good quality. This oil would be a splurge, but it's helpful for so many different things. I especially love it for Empaths because feelings of low self-worth, self-esteem, and feelings of loneliness, rejection, and abandonment are all common. Rose is incredibly uplifting to the mind, body, emotions, and spirit.

2) Frankincense
- Repels negativity
- Increases your sense of spirituality and self
- Calms anxiety and induces a sense of mental peace

Frankincense has been used for thousands of years and was even mentioned in the Bible as one of the gifts of the Wise Men. When used for mental/emotional purposes, it elevates the spirit and calms the mind. When you're swirling with anxiety, Frankincense helps you slow down, breathe, and re-group. If possible, you can diffuse it prior to any encounter or situation where you're anticipating stress or negativity.

Frankincense is considered a protection oil and will also remove negative entities from your aura and space. It can help you reach a meditative state and allows for a deeper connection to spirit. In this way, it's also an excellent grounding oil. It's associated with the crown chakra and helps open that chakra if it was closed due to trauma and fear.

3) Geranium
- Defends against negativity directed towards you
- Increases feelings of love and protection
- Helps relieve anxiety

Geranium helps release you from a fear of love itself. Once you embrace love, you're able to feel safe. It helps relieve stress and anxiety providing a calming effect. Geranium strengthens the spiritual body and keeps the aura safe. It keeps negativity away while raising your own vibration. Geranium helps you heal from heartbreak and get back to a place of self-love. It serves as an emotional balancer between aggression and passivity.

4) Basil
- Helps ease stress and increase mental clarity
- Increases self-confidence and motivation
- Provides energetic protection in crowds

Basil stimulates the mind and improves clarity and focus. Many Empaths have difficulty controlling their anxiety when in crowds. Basil keeps you grounded and feeling mentally clear when you're in crowded places. It gives you inner strength and courage to do the things you were previously afraid of, so you can pursue your heart's desire. Diffusing Basil essential oil in your home can clear out any negativity that may have collected there. It's known as a "protector of the family".

5) Melaleuca (Tea Tree)
- Protects you from spiritual parasites
- Helps establish boundaries in relationships
- Protecting and grounding

Tea tree is another essential oil that can fit into multiple categories. As a protection blend, it protects your energy from energetic vampires or spiritual parasites. It helps you establish firm boundaries in relationships where you may be dominated by a partner or boss. In these relationships, you can feel taken advantage of because it seems as if what you want doesn't matter. Tea tree can also help relieve the mental strain and fatigue that comes along with co-dependent or narcissistic relationships. In these relationships, it's common to feel stuck, depressed and like you've been repressed for too long. I chose to list it in the Protection section, but it's an equally powerful cleanser. Tea tree helps you release the experience of being a victim and restores your courage.

Journaling Exercise

It can be helpful to identify situations where you feel unsafe or where you could use extra shielding.

-What makes me feel unsafe?
-What boundaries do I need to draw in order to feel protected?
-What situations cause me the most anxiety? Why?
-Where am I giving my power away to others?

Cleansing

In my opinion, this is the most important step for Empaths to follow and it's **NON-OPTIONAL**! Empaths are like sponges and can absorb the feelings of others. If you don't cleanse, then all that emotional clutter builds up inside of you and can alter the make-up of your own emotions. So, this **MUST** be done daily. I learned this the hard way!

When I first began doing **Neuro-Emotional Technique (N.E.T.)** exclusively, it was about 6 months later that I felt my personality changing. I became negative, sad and depressed. I knew that I wasn't my typical self, but I couldn't figure out what was making me feel so bad. One day, a colleague asked if she could use my office to host a party where an intuitive would be giving readings. I agreed, and on the day of the party, I stopped by to say hello after my clients were finished. Well, this woman told me to sit down and asked me "What are you doing?!" I was puzzled and asked her what she meant. She said, "You have a grey band going across your solar plexus chakra. What do you do for work?". When I told her about **Neuro-Emotional Technique (N.E.T.)** she asked me where I sent the emotions after they were released. I told her "Nowhere. They just go away." because this topic wasn't addressed when I was learning the technique. She said, "Guess what? All those emotions went right into you!". It was at that moment that I began to realize the true power and destruction of absorbing the emotions of others without getting rid of them. She gave me a few exercises to clear the emotions away from my energy field, but it took a good 3 months of near daily work to complete.

Since then, I've become passionate about teaching others cleansing techniques so they can avoid what happened to me! Many people ask me how I'm able to avoid taking the deep emotional and traumatic issues of my clients home with me. I'm able to disengage because of the techniques I've discussed in this book. I've found that a good majority of Empaths will ground and protect on some level, but either don't know about cleansing or skip it completely. If this crucial step is skipped, then it's like putting on clothes day after day without ever taking any off. Pretty soon, you're not going to be very comfortable. Most of us consider our personal hygiene as important, so you shower and brush your teeth daily. Think of energetic cleansing as a vital part of your daily routine in much the same way.

Smudging

One of my favorite cleansing techniques is called smudging. There are many herbs or resins that can be used for this purpose. Sage is a popular choice and can be purchased in bundles or loose leaves. Light the sage and place it in a heat proof dish or bowl. Abalone sea shells are often used to hold the sage because it brings in the water element as an additional cleanser. As the smoke rises, you can use a fan (often a feather to represent the air element), or your hands to blow the smoke over yourself front and back. It's also a good idea to sage electronics and your home to make sure all the energy around you is cleansed. Some people perform elaborate ceremonies around smudging, but I personally don't think there is a "wrong" way to smudge. Simply hold the intention of cleansing yourself, your belongings, and your area.

Wood from the Palo Santo tree is another popular choice for smudging if you don't like or can't tolerate sage. It's sold in sticks approximately 2-3 inches long and you light them much the same way you would the sage. However, the Palo Santo wood does not produce much smoke making it ideal for cleansing small areas and for personal use. It has a light and woody scent that's incredibly sensual and uplifting. One of my clients mentioned that it always made her feel like she was in the jungle when she would come into my office. I like to burn Palo Santo at the beginning of my work day and between clients to make sure the energy of my room is nice and clean.

Resins such as Copal, Juniper, Frankincense and Myrrh can also be burnt for cleansing. However, these require the use of charcoal discs. They can be purchased online or in specialty shops. To use, place the discs inside a heat proof dish and light them. Be patient because they're very hard to light! When the disc turns grey, place the resin crystals on top. They will melt and release their fragrant cleansing smoke.

Native Americans would also use an herb called Sweetgrass. This herb is often lit after sage has been used to cleanse the area. Sweetgrass will "call in good spirits" to the area once the negativity has been cleared. The plant has a lovely sweet smell and is often sold in braided ropes. It's difficult to keep lit but the smell is heavenly!

Essential Oils for Cleansing

If you're unable to tolerate smoke, or in an environment where you can't burn anything, then you can make a smudging spray with essential oils. This is a great way to make sure that you're cleansed throughout your day in your work environment. Simply fill a 2-4 oz glass bottle with spring water, and a 5-10 drops of cleansing essential oils. Spray as needed to cleanse your energy. Here are a few suggestions of cleansing essential oils:

1) **Sage**
   - Purifies your aura and space
   - Stimulates the mind
   - Cleanses the heart and mind of negative influences

Although burning sage is one of my favorite ways to cleanse, it's not always possible to cleanse your environment this way. Making a Sage cleansing spray is an excellent and portable way to make sure that you're cleansed and protected in any situation. Cleansing the aura with Sage makes you feel immediately lighter. It stimulates your mind to begin creative processes that have been suppressed.

2) **Citrus oils: Orange, lemon, bergamot, grapefruit, lime, tangerine, mandarin**
   - Clears the mind
   - Uplifts the spirit
   - Unblocks stagnant energy

I decided to place the citrus scents together because of the similarities between them. Citrus scents are some of the very best oils for uplifting the spirit and elevating the mood. These oils are associated with the solar plexus and the sacral chakras. They are excellent at inspiring creativity, courage, and facilitating the smooth flow of energy throughout your body. When your energy is blocked, you can feel the following: fear, anger, frustration, shame, guilt, depressed, and stuck. If you've absorbed the negative energy of others, these oils provide the cleansing you need to restore your hope and optimism. It helps you forgive yourself and others while releasing the burdens you've been carrying.

3) Eucalyptus
- Uplifts the mood and banishes sadness
- Relieves the feeling that you are being restricted by life
- Encourages the healthy release of emotions

Eucalyptus is a heart healer. It opens the heart and helps you release stored emotions and trauma in a healthy way. When traumatic experiences and emotions are buried, the grief, anger, sadness, guilt and shame will express themselves in some way. Eucalyptus steers the release in a positive direction.

4) Lavender
- Opens the heart
- Calms the nervous system
- Balances the emotions

Lavender is one of the most popular essential oils because it's so versatile. When it comes to cleansing however, it helps you unload the burdens of your day and relax on every level. Its calming and relaxing energy works to open the heart and helps relieve sadness, depression, grief, and broken hearts. If you've been suffering from "disappointed love", then Lavender restores the ability to move forward and love again leaving behind the heaviness of grief and heartbreak.

Lavender is well known as a remedy for insomnia. It calms and soothes the nervous system allowing you to relax. The stresses of modern-day life cause the "switch" of the nervous system to get stuck in the sympathetic mode. When you're in this mode, you can suffer from ailments including insomnia, high blood pressure, anxiety attacks, and unexplained fear. This is because your mind and body are constantly looking for the next potential threat. Lavender is special because it calms the body, mind, and soothes the emotions while cleansing the spirit.

5) Clary Sage
- Cleanses the aura
- Removes negativity from your personal space
- Helps relieve sadness, fear, and paranoia

Clary sage is a powerful tonic to the nervous system. It helps calm anxiety, fear, and paranoia while uplifting the spirit. It's similar in action to Sage essential oil with more of an effect on the nervous system. Clary sage can also combat the nervous exhaustion that comes along with obsessively worrying about what you can't control.

6) Peppermint
- Raises the vibration of a space
- Helps you find your center
- Cleans the aura and increases intuition

Peppermint's uplifting scent raises the vibration of your environment while helping you stay alert. It works to increase your intuition and connect you with your center. Because Peppermint increases your awareness and intuition, it helps you release fears about the unknown. When you trust yourself, you remove doubts and fears about following the wrong path or making the wrong choices. By clearing emotions that don't belong to you and uplifting your spirit, you're better able to multi-task and focus with clarity and optimism.

Gemstones and Crystals for Cleansing

1) Sodalite
- Cleanses your energy of "emotional clutter"
- Helps calm anxiety
- Connects you with your intuition

Sodalite was the first energy cleansing gemstone that I learned about during my crystal healing journey. It cleanses the aura and removes the "emotional clutter" that you have absorbed throughout the day. It acts like a vacuum cleaner to remove all things that don't belong to you from your aura. When your energy is cleared of this clutter, it helps you release stored anxiety that may or may not belong to you. Sodalite is so powerful that it will also cleanse your space from EMF and negative energy. It's another gemstone that's fantastic if you're an energy worker or in an office where it's vital to keep the energy of your space clean and freely circulating. Because it corresponds to the brow or third eye chakra, it can help deepen your intuition, inspire creativity, allows a deeper connection with spirit, and clears the mind of "mental clutter".

2) Shungite
- Helps restore emotional balance
- Absorbs negative energy and EMF pollution
- Helps remove negative influences from your life

Shungite is another stone that does triple duty between grounding, protection, and cleansing. It helps remove negative people and influences from your life. Not only will it cleanse your energy of negativity, but it will also help repel negativity from even reaching you! By removing negative people, influences, and energy from your life, you're bound to feel an upswing in your mood and optimism. Shungite is another EMF cleanser and can keep your home or office environment clear. Place a piece near your computer, microwave, and router to cleanse your energy.

3) Selenite
- Promotes harmony and peaceful energy
- Cleanses the aura of negativity
- Opens blocked chakras

Selenite is known as Liquid Light and is named after the Greek goddess of the moon, Selene. It cleanses the mind and helps reduce scattered thoughts so you can focus. It strengthens the mind and prevents against psychic attacks. Selenite also opens the chakras and removes blocked energies. When your energy is flowing freely, you begin to radiate a higher frequency and become more attuned to love. Selenite can also be used to strengthen romantic relationships between partners by cleansing their energy and returning them to love.

Placing your feet on Selenite wands can shift and cleanse your energy within 20 minutes! To keep your living and workspace clean, place Selenite at each corner of the room. To remove negativity and cleanse your personal energy, you can wave a Selenite wand up and down your body.

4) Clear Quartz
- Repairs and replenishes the aura
- Amplifies the energy of other crystals
- Filters negativity and transforms harsh words

Clear Quartz is known as an amplifier and will increase the effectiveness and energy of other crystals. It can be programmed with a particular intention, and even used in a pinch if you need the healing properties of another crystal but don't have one available. Clear Quartz is unique in that it can mimic the energy of any other crystal for a short period of time when programmed. It cleanses you of inner negativity and helps you reach a more positive state. This is especially helpful if you engage in negative self-talk. It cleanses the mind and brings you peace from negative thoughts. Clear Quartz can enhance your communication with your guardian angels and is used in Feng Shui to disperse the sun's energy throughout a room.

Because it carries the light ray of every color, it can be used to clear and align all the chakras. It repels and cleanses the negativity from energy vampires and dark intentions. It helps revitalize the energy and the mind.

5) Citrine
- Absorbs and transmutes negative energy
- Rejuvenates the spirit
- Increases optimism, energy and drive

When you've been exposed to negative energy, it causes you to feel and think negatively. If it's not cleansed, this negative frame of mind can cause a downward spiral in your personality and outlook on life. Citrine is a great cleansing stone for this situation. It corresponds to the solar plexus chakra, improves your self-esteem, and raises your spirit. When you've absorbed too much toxic energy, it's often hard to BEGIN making the necessary changes to cleanse and shift. Citrine brings a ray of sunlight to the aura and propels you out of that yucky place that's been making you feel stuck. It gives you the drive and inspiration to pull yourself out of the funk.

6) **Sugilite**
   - Removes negative attachments and blockages in the aura
   - Enhances psychic and natural abilities
   - Encourages you to let go of worry and pain

Sugilite is like a giant vacuum cleaner for negative energy! My first experience with Sugilite was during a gemstone healing session. When a Sugilite sphere was held over my liver, I felt a pulling sensation as negative energy was sucked out of my liver into the gem. It was powerful!

Sugilite helps you release stored anger, fear, bitterness and sorrow. If you feel as if the world has become too intense and your burdens are too heavy, then consider Sugilite. It helps you let go of the weight of the world and reconnect with unconditional love. It's also an excellent stone for children if they're feeling unsafe or suffering from nightmares.

It's associated with the Crown Chakra and the development of psychic or intuitive abilities. Sugilite can be used during the Violet Flame Cleansing Technique to burn away dark or negative spots in your aura. If mental worry is a problem, then Sugilite can help you get in touch with your optimism.

7) Black Kyanite
- Opens the mind
- Aligns the chakras
- Dispels blocked energy

When your energy field has blockages, it's easy to feel down on yourself or even fall into thinking that things are never going to get better. Negative energy causes negative thinking and it can easily lead to a place of feeling disempowered or even like a victim. Black Kyanite restores the normal flow of your energy and allows the mind to reach a more optimistic state. It's also a grounding stone and corresponds to the Root Chakra.

As we've previously explored, the Root Chakra deals with safety. Black Kyanite is another stone that makes you feel safe, protected, and empowered. This is especially helpful if you feel "out of place" in your environment. Black Kyanite can help you make difficult decisions and enhance your intuitive gifts.

Because Black Kyanite is protecting and grounding as well, it can be used to re-align your chakras and is an excellent stone to perform cord cutting rituals (more on this later). You can use a spear of Black Kyanite like a wand and run it up and down your body. The stone will be drawn to any pockets of negativity or blocked chakras. Begin over your head and move the spear slowly downward. If you feel any resistance to the downward flow, then simply pause at that place until you feel drawn to move the spear downward again. This will open your chakras and allow your energy to flow freely. This same exercise can be performed in a similar manner with the intention of cord cutting.

Cleansing Your Crystals

It's a good idea to cleanse your gemstones and crystals after they've done their job of cleansing you! There are several methods of keeping your gemstones cleansed, and some will be better than others depending on the composition of your crystal. For example, Selenite will dissolve if placed in water! When in doubt, do a quick internet search on how to cleanse your individual crystals, or choose the least invasive method as possible. For best results, try to clean your gemstones at least 3 times per week to keep them fully charged and working their best. If you're going through an intensely emotional time or in a toxic environment, then your stones may need daily cleansing.

Here are a few ways to cleanse your crystals.

Sunlight:

Sunlight is one of the easiest ways to cleanse your stones because it's readily available. Simply leave them in sunlight for 5-10 minutes for lighter colored crystals such as Rose Quartz or Amethyst. Darker stones can be left up to an hour.

Water Bath:

Water is an amazing cleanser! This method is great if you're traveling, during the winter, or on rainy days when your bright sunlight is limited. In this method, you run them under alternating hot and cold water. I place my stones in a strainer so that they're easily contained while I run the basket under a stream of water. If using this method, then do 3 cycles of hot/cold and end the treatment with cold water. However, some gems and crystals don't tolerate water well, so make sure yours are water safe!

Salt Bed:

Salt is an excellent cleanser (more on that later)! If you're unsure about whether your crystals can tolerate water, then you can place them on top of a bed of salt. The salt should be about 1-2 inches thick in a glass or porcelain bowl. Place a cotton cloth on top of the salt to protect your crystals. You can use the salt for 1-2 weeks before it needs to be replaced. Salt can be corrosive to some crystals especially when set in jewelry, so make sure your stones only touch the cloth.

Salt Scrubs and Baths

I love salt scrubs! These are so easy to make and it's something you can do with your kids as a fun activity. They can also be wonderful gifts for all the other Empaths in your life. Not only will scrubs cleanse you physically, but energetically as well! The crystalline matrix of salt (or sugar) absorbs negative energy. So, when you're feeling like you've had a "bad Empath day", simply scrub or soak away other people's energy that has attached to you. I try to do salt scrubs or baths several times a week. If you have difficulty carving out enough "me" time for the baths or simply don't like them, then the scrubs are the best quick and easy alternative. Any kind of salt can be used for the scrub, but I generally use Epsom salt. Celtic sea salt or a mix of both. If you decide to use sugar, choose a type with larger crystals so that it doesn't melt too quickly.

Here's my recipe:

- **1 cup Epsom Salt**
- **1-2 Tablespoons oil**
- **2-3 drops essential oil**

Mix together all ingredients and place in a container that would be safe in the shower. This recipe makes enough for 2-4 treatments.

I tend to use Grapeseed, Avocado, Almond, or Apricot oil for my scrubs. If you don't have access to those, then you can use olive oil as well. Coconut oil (unless you use a fractionated form) isn't necessarily the best choice because it becomes solid in cooler temperatures and will be difficult to spread. You can choose from the cleansing essential oils in this section, or any other that you prefer.

If you would rather take a salt bath versus a scrub, add about **2 cups** of Epsom salt to your bath water. If you would like to add essential oils to your bath, you may want to dilute them first in a small amount of carrier oil. Otherwise, they may not dilute well in your bath water and some essential oils are considered "hot" oils meaning they may irritate your skin if not diluted properly.

Cord Cutting

If you've never heard of cord cutting, then you're not alone. Cords are energetic connections that attach between people that interact with each other. These interactions can be fleeting lasting only moments or from long term relationships. Here's an extra kicker, now that we're in a digital age, these connections can be virtual as well! Think about how many people you interact with on social media platforms. In addition, if you make (or even watch) videos for a product or service then everyone who views them is interacting with you energetically! Now, can you imagine the number of cords you might be carrying? Staggering right?! So, let's get rid of them!

Settle yourself into a comfortable position. In your mind, visualize your body. Can you see any cords or ropes that may be attached to you? These can be any length, thickness, or color and can be attached to any location on your body. You may also be able to see who is attached to the other end. Now, imagine yourself cutting these cords. You can either pull them out or use swords, knives, scissors or any kind of blade to make these cuts. I like to imagine cutting both ends of the cords between me and the other person. Depending on how long cords have been attached and who is on the other end, this ritual may need to be performed several times before you're finally "clean". I also like to imagine a green healing light where the cord was to seal over the "wound" that was there. It's important to note that we are cutting cords of low vibration or negativity. Some people worry that cord cutting will alienate you from your loved ones. However, cords that are forged of a pure and true love will continue to stay. It's only those that aren't for your best and highest good that will be cleared away.

Cord cutting is essential for Empaths to do on a regular basis. Energy vampires are often narcissistic people who are extremely attracted to an Empath's healing, loving, and compassionate energy. These vampires will often make you feel drained because they're stealing your energy through a cord connection. Basically, you're like a giant juice box and they're sucking you dry through these cordlike straws. When you disconnect from these vampires, a few things may happen. You (or they) may feel an empty sensation and this can feel very disconcerting. It's a temporary feeling, and as long as you stay shielded, it'll go away. However, the vampire panics at this empty feeling and will attempt to reattach the cord to get their hooks into you again. Because of this, grounding, shielding, and cleansing are important to practice CONSISTENTLY. You may also discover that when you cut cords to some people, they'll attempt to contact you physically. For example, when you cord cut an ex out of your life, don't be surprised if they begin calling, coming around or emailing again because they're missing the constant energy flow!

Here's a technique that I do nightly to make cord cutting even more powerful. It's become a nighttime ritual of mine to make sure that my energy is cleansed and cleared before I go to sleep at night. Simply ask (God, Source, Universe, Angels, Jesus, etc…whoever you feel comfortable with) or imagine that if anyone has taken your energy over the course of the day, it be extracted from them, cleansed and returned to you. Also, if you've absorbed or taken anyone else's energy over the course of the day, that it be extracted from you, cleansed

48

and returned to them. In this way, everyone is ending the day with the energy they started it with all cleansed and purified.

Strengthening Your Personal Boundaries with Flower Essences

Empaths respond very well to flower essence therapy. Flower essences are different from essential oils and often work on a person energetically. They are meant to be placed in water and sipped throughout the day. The essences will help you strengthen yourself in a gentle, yet effective way. Here are several that I feel would benefit Empaths. Every Empath will be at a different part of their journey and will have different needs. You can choose several from this list, but no more than seven at a time is advised. Two reputable companies are Flower Essence Services (FES) or Bach Flower Remedies. The essences can be combined in a glass dropper bottle with spring water and a preservative such as brandy or apple cider vinegar. These essences can take up to 3 months for full benefit, so be patient!

Here's a tip: Almost every Empath that I know **NEEDS** Centaury! This is because Empaths tend to be extremely giving often to their detriment. Also, you may be out of touch with your own wants and needs. Based on your upbringing, you may have learned what you wanted didn't matter because you wouldn't get it anyway. Centaury is an excellent remedy to start with if you feel overwhelmed reading the flowers listed below and don't know where to begin.

-**Mimulus:** Excessive anxiety and nervousness about daily life, everyday fears, having a fretful and fearful attitude, shyness

-**Red Chestnut:** Bringing calm but caring detachment when others are in need. Counteracting over-concern and obsessive worry for others

-**Sagebrush:** Holding on to false identity and life circumstances which are no longer appropriate

-**Garlic:** Releasing nervous fears and insecurities that weaken the life force, protection from psychic parasites which drain one's vitality

-**Pink Yarrow:** Tendency to be an emotional sponge, absorbing emotional qualities of others, leading to emotional oversensitivity, no longer in touch with one's own feelings and boundaries, emotional vulnerability, the need for emotional centering and strength, internalizing others' problems as if they were your own

-**Corn:** Centeredness in crowded environments such as cities, grounded spirituality related to the Earth, finding one's spiritual roots

-**Golden Yarrow:** Ability to set aside personal anxiety or sensitivity when needing to focus on an outer activity

-**Indian Pink:** Keeping a still center in the midst of intense activity or pressure

-**Red Clover:** Keeping calm and centered in challenging circumstances, especially when others are emotionally upset and unbalanced

-**Centaury:** Unhealthy need to serve or please others, unbalanced giving which weakens and depletes the true self, accepting exploitation from others, excessive obligation to the needs of others, becoming drained and depleted rather than replenished by healing work, wanting to be of service but must find inner balance between other' and own needs, knowing one's limits in sharing with others, the ability to say "NO" when appropriate

-**Elm:** Knowing one is capable of fulfilling one's obligations without anxiety

-**Buttercup:** Knowing self-worth, especially with regard to vocation and lifestyle, belittling oneself, shyness about sharing one's gifts with others

-**Golden Yarrow:** Confidence that one can perform despite anxiety and oversensitivity, helping oneself stay connected and receptive to others, despite sensitivity, ability to remain open to others while still feeling inner protection

-**Fawn Lily:** Strength to give oneself to the world, despite innate desire to retreat, highly sensitive and spiritually attuned, but often feeling fatigued or drained by work, feeling one's work is chaotic or stressful, preferring retreat or isolation

-**Yarrow:** Over-absorption of others' suffering, resulting in feelings of depletion, need for more psychic detachment, bringing more light and strength in the aura to overcome feelings of vulnerability, protection from negative thoughts or environmental influences, need for protection, overly porous auric field

-**Tansy:** Suppression of one's energy and feelings in order to keep the peace, or to deal with emotional overwhelm

-**Aspen:** Hypersensitive to things unseen or unknown, need for psychic balance

Conclusion

The world needs YOU as an Empath. It needs your love, dedication, compassion, and your ability to help others heal. I hope this book has shown you that you are incredibly powerful! You can feel even more so by utilizing some basic techniques provided in this book for your safety and comfort. It's not selfish to allow yourself to receive healing, empowerment, and love. Through your own healing journey, you'll learn valuable techniques to uplift and heal others. In the Law of Attraction, we tend to attract people who need to recover from the same things that we've already dealt with in the past. This is an incredible strength! When you overcome low self-esteem, a lack of confidence, depression, and anxiety, YOU become the guide to help someone else along their journey. Therefore, times of great pain can be transformed into an incredible healing force.

It's my greatest wish that you find that place within you that feels whole, healthy, and complete. As humans, sometimes things can get tough, and Earth isn't always the easiest place. Just remember, there are an army of Empaths all over the planet doing the same work as you. Lean on your brother and sister healers when you need it, and someday you'll be able to return the healing favor to someone else. In this way, you practice a balanced system of giving and receiving which allows you to thrive.

I'm sending you so much love, strength and blessings. You are amazing! Thank you for reading my book, and please share it with your friends, family and loved ones who need the healing contained inside.

Carry on with all your healing brilliance, Empaths!!!!

About the Author

 Dr. April Darley is a Naturopathic Doctor specializing in a revolutionary non-drug therapy called **Neuro-Emotional Technique (N.E.T.).** After suffering a debilitating back injury, she healed with alternative therapies after releasing trapped emotions using **Neuro-Emotional Technique (N.E.T.).** This experience was so powerful, she dedicated her entire practice to helping people with anxiety, pain, trauma, and stress by using this transformative technique. Dr. Darley became passionate about helping people suffering with anxiety regain confidence, happiness, and the ability to move forward from situations keeping them stuck.

After several years of helping others through **Neuro-Emotional Technique (N.E.T.)**, she began combining this revolutionary therapy with proven success strategies to bring about a truly transformational experience for her clients. This combination uncovers subconscious patterns that have caused self-sabotaging behaviors and gives you the opportunity for complete freedom and empowerment.

If you need help releasing trauma and trapped emotions affecting your behavior, then consider **Neuro-Emotional Technique (N.E.T.).** You can find more information about **Neuro-Emotional Technique (N.E.T.)** by visiting www.evolvenaturalwellness.com. Dr. Darley treats clients by appointment in the Dallas-Fort Worth area of Texas, or by video for clients all over the world.

Join me on social media at:

https://www.facebook.com/draprildarley/
https://www.facebook.com/EvolveNaturalWellness/
https://www.instagram.com/draprildarley/

Join my exclusive Empath Support Group at:

https://www.facebook.com/groups/empoweredhealers/

Made in the USA
Las Vegas, NV
27 November 2024